Walking in
Hampshire

Walking in Hampshire

Twenty four country rambles based on
the County Recreation Department's
popular programme of Guided Walks

COUNTRYSIDE BOOKS
NEWBURY BERKSHIRE

First Published 1984
© Hampshire County Council 1984
Updated 1986

ISBN 0 905392 33 7

Designed by Mon Mohan
Cover photograph by Hampshire County Council Recreation Department

Produced through MRM (Print Consultants) Ltd., Reading, Berkshire.

Printed in England by Riverside Press, Reading, Berkshire.

Sketch Map of Hampshire showing locations of the walks~

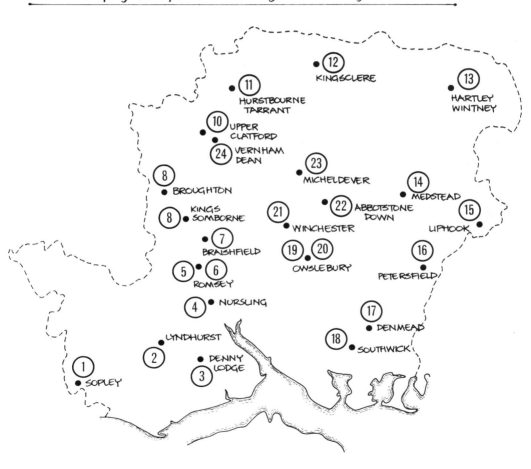

Introduction

Since the summer of 1981 Hampshire County Council's Recreation Department has produced a series of leaflets under the general title of "Discover Hampshire – Guided Walks". These have listed hundreds of walks in all parts of the county in both summer and winter with the object of providing both residents and visitors with the opportunity to explore Hampshire's marvellously varied countryside. All the walks have been led by volunteers who have been drawn from Parish Councils, local societies, the Ramblers' Association and other walking clubs as well as the Recreation Department's own staff. Each leader chose his own route, his own time and date and it was then simply a matter of waiting to see who, if anyone, would come along.

The response in 1981 was encouraging with some 90 walks attracting nearly 2000 people. Since then numbers of both walks and participants have increased and the 'Discover Hampshire – Guided Walks' programme is now firmly established as a regular feature among the Department's promotions.

Many of those who tried country walking, perhaps for the first time, on these guided walks have become regular 'customers' and have later returned and walked some of the routes with friends or on their own.

One of the original walks was published in a local Parish Magazine in the form of a sketch map with additional information. This seemed such a splendid idea that we have now put together a number of original 'Discover Hampshire' walks in this book. Our thanks are due to David Clark of Liphook for agreeing that we can use his idea and to the other volunteer leaders who have contributed their efforts to the book. Now anyone can explore some of the best walking in Hampshire in their own time and at their own pace

However, for those who like to be shown the way, the Department's leaflets of guided walks are published twice yearly in April and October and are obtainable through libraries, Information Offices or direct from the County Recreation Department at North Hill Close, Andover Road, Winchester. For those who would like to extend their walking activities there are one-week walking holidays organised by the Recreation Department each summer, details of which are available in January each year.

The sketch map that accompanies each walk in this book is designed to guide walkers to the starting point and give a simple but accurate idea of the route to be taken. For those who like the benefit of detailed maps the relevant Ordnance Survey 1:50,000 series sheet is recommended.

Finally, may I say thank you to all the volunteers who, since 1981, have given their services to make the 'Discover Hampshire' programmes possible and to Countryside Books of Newbury who have undertaken the task of putting this book together.

W.A. BIDE
SENIOR RIGHTS OF WAY OFFICER
HAMPSHIRE COUNTY RECREATION DEPARTMENT

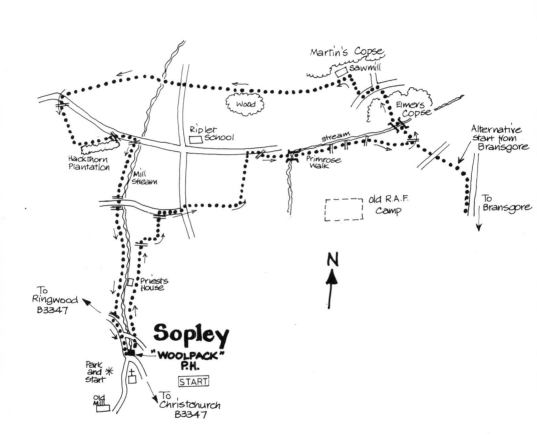

Martin's Copse
sawmill
Wood
Elmers Copse
Ripler School
stream
Alternative start from Bransgore
Hackthorn Plantation
Mill Stream
Primrose Walk
old R.A.F. Camp
To Bransgore
To Ringwood B3347
Priests House
N
Sopley
"WOOLPACK" P.H.
Park and start
START
Old Mill
To Christchurch B3347

WALK 1
AROUND SOPLEY
– distance 5 miles (2½ hours)

Introduction
The Hampshire Avon has its source in the Wiltshire Downs, flows near the western boundaries of the New Forest and then through a quiet valley before entering the English Channel at Christchurch Bay. In this valley lies the pleasant village of Sopley with its surrounding farmlands, little streams and woods. This walk is over level countryside and suitable for walking all year.

How to get there
Coming from Christchurch (B3347) turn left over the bridge opposite the Woolpack PH. Approaching from Ringwood (B3347) pass through Sopley along the one-way road and straight over the bridge. Start reference 157 967. This walk can also be made from Bransgore, parking behind the shops and walking north to a footpath as shown.

Points of Interest
SOPLEY VILLAGE: contains some most interesting buildings. There is a PRIEST HOUSE located on a very old lane which used to run to North Ripley. It has a priest hole that was used during the Reformation. The WOOLPACK INN was used to collect tolls before the bridge was built. Opposite the FORGE is the OLD VILLAGE WASH HOUSE and in Derrith Lane a 13th century SADDLE BEAM can be seen.
THE OLD MILL: which stands by the river Avon near the church belonged to the monks of Christchurch, having been granted them in 1146, and here they are said to have had their infirmary.
ST MICHAEL'S CHURCH: This is a 13th century church built in a pre-Saxon mound. Built of ironstone from Hengistbury

Head, it has effigies of Purbeck Marble on either side of the north door, thought to be of the founders of the church. Originally recumbent, they were transferred to their present position to preserve them from further damage. In the churchyard is the tomb of LORD KEANE who led the march to Kabul in the Afghan War in 1839, and whose force was cut to pieces in the Khyber Pass. There is also a War Memorial Tablet by the well-known early 20th century artist ERIC GILL.

ST CATHERINES HILL: Looking south from the church there is a lovely view down the tree-fringed river Avon to the estuary and to St Catherines Hill. On the hill are remains of large Bronze Age round barrows and on the south-west side can be traced the foundations of the ancient chapel of St Catherine, the virgin martyr of Alexandria, reputed to have been broken on the wheel and then beheaded in the year 307. Early Crusaders brought the legend to Europe, the earliest reference in England being a Miracle Play about her, first performed in Dunstable in 1100.

TYRRELLS FORD: Two miles north of the village is the ford, according to local tradition the very one (of many claimants) through which Walter Tyrrell rode after the murder of William Rufus, on his way to take ship for France.

Submitted by: Mr N Chapman
58 Hinton Wood Avenue
Highcliffe
Christchurch

WALK 2
BOLDRE AND SETLEY PONDS
– distance 5 miles (2½ hours)

Introduction
Few places can rival the New Forest for providing so varied a landscape within so small an area – deep thick woodland, windswept heathland and riverside glades. Its combination of climate, position and size make it a haven for wildlife, birds and plants; their study and conservation. This walk passes through the picturesque village of Boldre with its delightful thatched cottages, and begins at nearby Setley Ponds.

How to get there
Boldre lies on the A337 between Lymington to the south and Brockenhurst to the north, and can be approached from Beaulieu on the B3055.

Points of Interest
BOLDRE CHURCH: Originally Norman with some 13th centrury additions, its upper stage is of brick and dated 1697. The church door key is said to have come from Beaulieu Abbey at the time of the Dissolution of the Monasteries.

HMS HOOD: The Memorial chapel commemorates the sinking of the *Hood* on 24 may 1941 off the Icelandic coast. Vice Admiral L.E. Holland worshipped regularly at the church and the chapel with its Book of Remembrance was set up by his widow.

ROYDEN MANOR: A 17th century manor house where W.H. Hudson, the famous naturalist spent some of his happiest Hampshire days. In the woods about it he saw "a hornet and a field vole dispute the ownership of a stream of elm sap".

WILLIAM GILPIN: The famous author of natural history books which included *Forest Scenery* was vicar of Boldre for 30 years until his death in 1804. A former headmaster of Cheam school, he first saw his parishioners as 'exposed to every temptation of pillage and robbery from their proximity to the deer, the game and the fuel of the Forest, these poor people were little better than *banditti'*. Indeed, the village's nearness to the 'Chines' of the coast at Lymington made it an ideal place for the storage of smuggled goods too. But what Charles Kingsley had yet to do for Eversley, William Gilpin did for Boldre.

An exceptional man, he devoted much of the proceeds of his best selling books to the welfare of his parishioners, reorganising the poorhouse and establishing a village school. He lived at VICARS HILL and upon his death the grateful

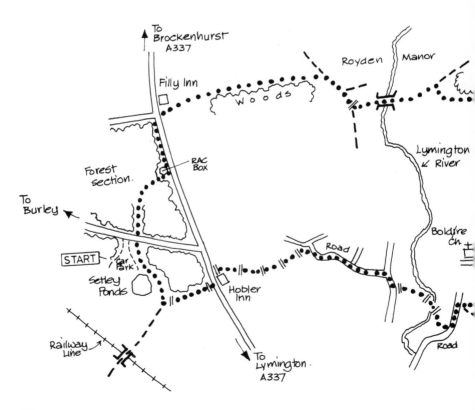

villagers erected a mural monument to his memory in the north aisle of the church, which speaks highly of the regard in which they must have held him.

ROBERT SOUTHEY: The 19th century Romantic poet was married in Boldre church to his second wife CAROLINE BOWLES in 1839. She returned to Boldre after Southey's death in Keswick three years later to live at BUCKLAND COTTAGE.

Submitted by: Mr D B Watton
1 Welbury Close
Lymington

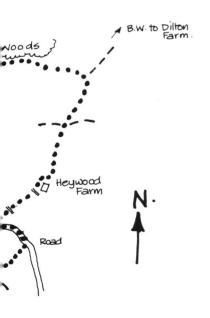

 stile or gate

WALK 3
DENNY LODGE
– distance 3½ miles (1½ hours)

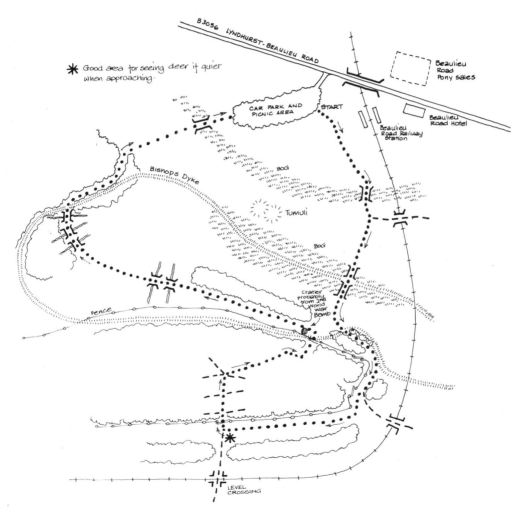

Introduction

A beautiful stretch of moorland lies in this part of the New Forest area, with great woodlands towards the western edge. The walk skirts the edge of the wood where deer may be seen.

How to get there

The walk begins at the picnic area and car park near Beaulieu Road railway station on the B3056 between Lyndhurst and Beaulieu.

Points of Interest

BISHOPS DYKE: The story goes that the king granted 'as much land in the New Forest as the Bishop of Winchester could crawl round on his hands and knees in a day'. Unfortunately for him this particular bishop was an athlete and sportsman. He chose the best bit of snipe shooting land in the Forest, interpreted the instruction as 24 hours, not 'in daylight', and crawled round a goodly area. It is interesting to note the similarity between this legend and another Hampshire 'crawl' – the one which created the Tichborne Dole. The more mundane explanation of the dyke is that the irregular shape of the marshy ground suggests that the dyke was built to enclose a shallow pond.

WOODFIDLEY: Just beyond Bishops Dyke to the south west. Lyndhurst people have a saying that if rain clouds come from that direction there will be 'Woodfidley rain' – steady and drenching all day long. It must have special powers for the same proverb holds true for the people of Brockenhurst and Beaulieu in two other directions!

Submitted by: Mr P Samphire
13 Knightwood Road
Hythe
Southampton

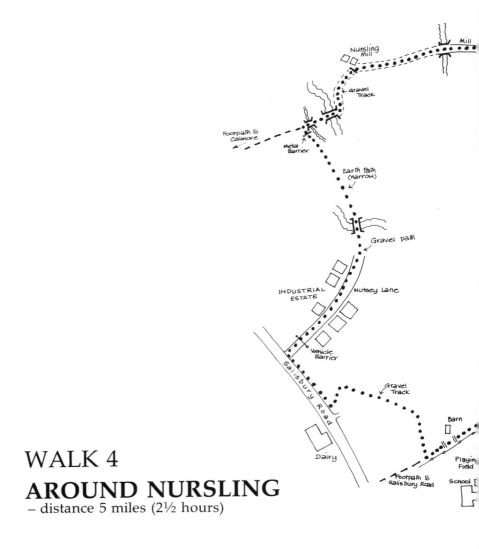

WALK 4
AROUND NURSLING
– distance 5 miles (2½ hours)

Introduction
This walk passes through the Lower Test Nature Reserve,
noted for its flora and fauna. The reserve is administered by
the Hampshire and Isle of Wight Naturalist Trust. At times
the marshes may be rather muddy and wellington boots are
advisable.

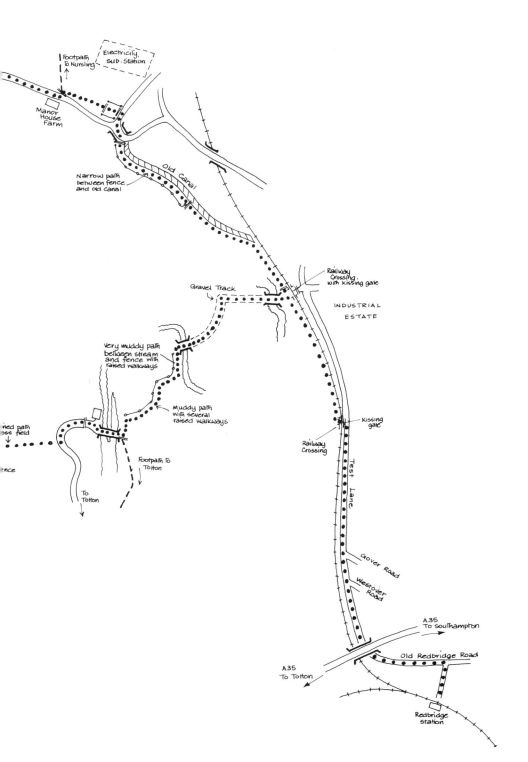

Footpath
To Nursling

Electricity
Sub-Station

Manor
House
Farm

Old Canal

Narrow path
between fence
and old canal

Railway
Crossing
with kissing gate

Gravel Track

INDUSTRIAL
ESTATE

Very muddy path
between stream
and fence with
raised walkways

Muddy path
with several
raised walkways

...ned path
...oss field

...nce

Footpath To
Totton

To
Totton

Kissing
gate

Railway
Crossing

Test Lane

Gover Road

Westover
Road

A35
To Southampton

A35
To Totton

Old Redbridge Road

Redbridge
Station

How to get there

Nursling lies just off the A35 between Totton and Southampton. The walk begins at Redbridge Station, a connecting point for trains and Hants and Dorset bus services, though the walk may be joined at any point on route.

Points of Interest

NURSLING VILLAGE: A scattered community by the river Test, that Mecca for fishermen, fed by streams swift and pure from the chalk downs, well-known for the abundance of its trout.

ST BONIFACE: Nursling is the site of a monastery from which St Boniface went forth to convert the Germans to Christianity in the 8th century, one of the most important acts of evangelism in European history. The Danes destroyed the monastery which probably stood in the vicinity of the present church.

Submitted by: Mr D Wallis
140 Ringwood Road
Totton
Southampton

WALK 5
TWO WALKS AROUND DUNBRIDGE
– distance North walk 7.25km. (2½ hours)
South walk 4km. (1½ hours)

Introduction
The north walk is mainly across open farmland, passing Mottisfont Abbey, while the south walk makes an appetising 'before lunch' walk with splendid views across farmland.

How to get there
The village of Dunbridge is on the B3084 road from Middle Wallop via Lockerley which connects with the A3057 Stockbridge to Romsey road on the eastern side of Mottisfont Abbey.

Points of Interest
MOTTISFONT ABBEY: Open to the public – April-End September only. Grounds open daily except Good Friday, Sunday and Monday, 2.30 pm-6.00 pm. House open Wednesday and Saturday 2.30 pm-6.00 pm. Cellerarium and Whistler Room only.

Originally an Augustinain Priory founded in 1201. At the Dissolution of the Monasteries it went to Lord Sandys, a gift from Henry VIII in exchange for the villages of Chelsea and Paddington. The house was given to the National Trust in 1957.

The masterpiece of the Abbey is a large sitting room created in the 1930s and decorated by Rex Whistler, the English painter and designer of stage sets. In the park-like garden there is a beautiful spring from which flows a clear stream to join the Test. Many specimens of fine trees can be seen here, including London Planes and Cedars of Lebanon. Also in the grounds there is a large ice-house, one of only a few in Hampshire.

In a stable courtyard the museum of the village and nearby area is well worth a visit, as is the special walled garden laid out by Graham Thomas as a show place for the National Trust's collection of historic roses.

Submitted by: Mr R G Genge
3 Linden Road
Romsey

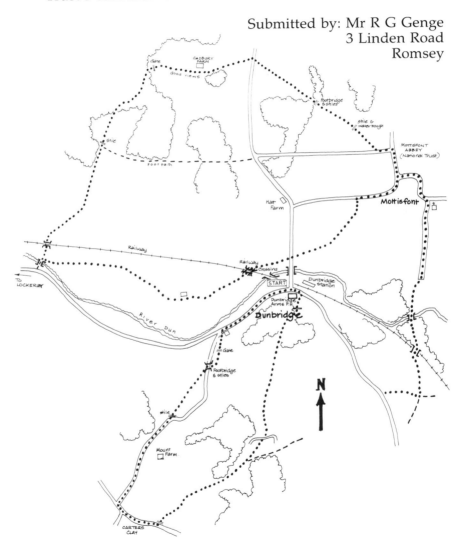

Walked
Sunday 7/2/88
V. N. L. G.

WALK 6
FROM ROMSEY RAILWAY STATION
– distance 12 km. (3½ hours)

Introduction
The pleasant market town of Romsey is built around the many streams of the river Test. This walk, just to the north of the town, is over level countryside. It passes Romsey Abbey and includes a quietly beautiful stretch by the canal.

How to get there
Romsey lies at the junction of several main routes through Hampshire; the A31 Winchester to Ringwood road, the A3057 Stockbridge to Southampton road, and the A27 Botley to Salisbury road. The walk's start is The Railway Station. The circuit is completed by walking from The Abbey through the town centre via The Hundred and Station Road.

Points of Interest
ROMSEY ABBEY: Open daily throughout the year 9.30 am-5.30 pm. Founded in 907, it was one of the leading Religious Houses of the Middle Ages. The nuns were great teachers, and many Royal and noble families sent their daughters to the Abbey for their education. However, the Black Death in the 14th century decimated the population and the glory of the Abbey declined and never completely recovered. At the Dissolution the church was bought by the town for £100 as a parish church and so saved from demolition.

There are many details of interest within the Abbey including a Saxon rood, medieval wall paintings and a 16th century reredos. The grave of Earl Mountbatten of Burma, murdered by terrorists in Ireland, bears the simple words 'In honour bound'.

SADDLERS MILL: Salmon are the fish of the lower Test, and

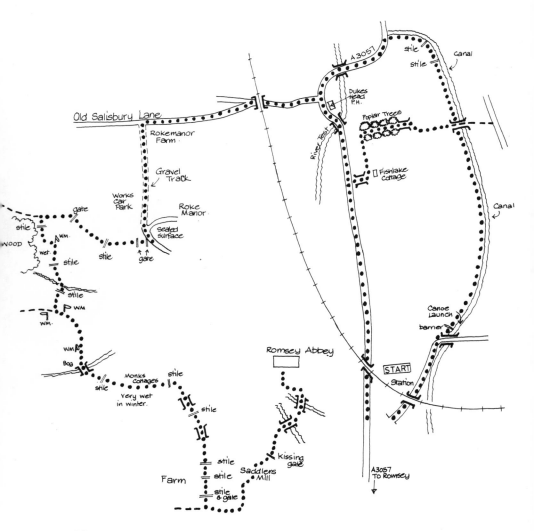

Old Salisbury Lane

A 3057

stile
stile
canal

Dukes Head P.H.

Rokemanor Farm

Poplar Trees

Fishlake Cottage

Gravel Track

River Test

Works Car Park

Roke Manor

Sealed Surface

gate

Canal

stile
WOOD
wet
WM.
stile

stile

gate

stile

WM

WM.

Canoe Launch

barrier

WM

Bog

stile

Monks Cottages

stile

Very wet in winter.

Romsey Abbey

START

Station

stile

stile

Kissing gate

Saddlers Mill

Farm

stile

stile

stile & gate

A3057 To Romsey

22

the 'Salmon leap' at the weir of Saddlers Mill is an annual attraction for residents and visitors when the fish return in November-December, leaping high against the tumbling water before laying their eggs in the river of their birth.
CANAL: ran from Andover to Redbridge and was in commercial use for 65 years until 1874.

Submitted by: Mr R G Genge
3 Linden Road
Romsey

WALK 7
AROUND BRAISHFIELD
– distance 5.5 km. (2½ hours)

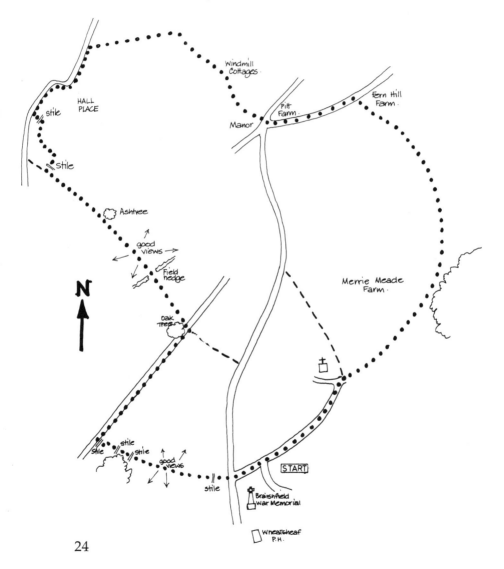

Introduction
This walk is over open farmland, suitable for walking in all seasons, and gives some panoramic views of the beautiful Test valley.

How to get there
The village of Braishfield lies about 2 miles from Romsey just off the A31 Romsey to Winchester road. Going north from Romsey, it will be found off to the right on the A3057 Stockbridge road, through Michelmersh.

Points of Interest
BRAISHFIELD VILLAGE: On the slopes which sweep up from the network of lanes is the site of perhaps the oldest building in England – a mesolithic house some 8,500 years old was discovered by keen archaeologist Mr Michael O'Malley. His work won him a BBC *Chronicle* award in 1979. The village boasts at least two ghosts – an Edwardian lady said to be looking for her jewels, and an apparition seen in the branches of an old yew tree near a deserted farmhouse.

BRAISHFIELD MANOR: An attractive early Georgian brick building with the recent addition of projecting two-bay wings.

Submitted by: Mr R G Genge
3 Linden Road
Romsey

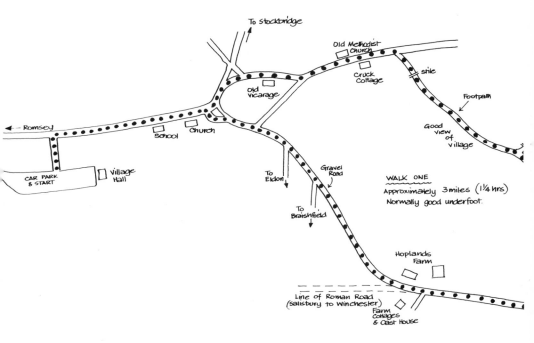

WALK 8
AROUND KINGS SOMBORNE
– distance 7 miles (3½ hours)

Introduction
This figure-of-eight walk may also be tackled as two shorter walks. The northern end of the 'eight' passes various interesting buildings of the village, while the southern circle gives excellent views of the surrounding countryside.

How to get there
Kings Somborne is on the A3057 Stockbridge to Romsey road, just south of Stockbridge.

Points of Interest

KINGS SOMBORNE VILLAGE: Here John of Gaunt had his palace in the 14th century. A King's manor in Domesday, Somborne was granted to William Briwere in 1190. King John often stayed with him here while hunting in the Forest which stretched away to the Itchen valley. There is a mutilated stone figure of William Briwere at the PARISH CHURCH. The

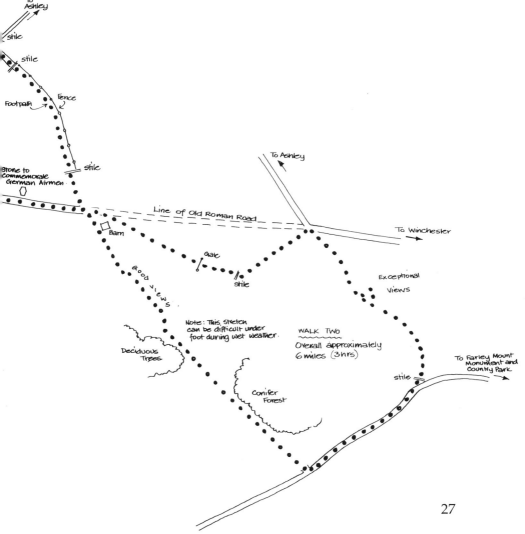

To Ashley

stile

stile

Footpath

Fence

stile

Stone to commemorate German Airmen

Line of Old Roman Road

To Ashley

To Winchester

Barn

Gate

stile

Exceptional Views

Good views

Note: This stretch can be difficult under foot during wet weather.

WALK TWO
Overall approximately 6 miles (3hrs)

Deciduous Trees

Conifer Forest

stile

To Farley Mount Monument and Country Park

church was restored in 1885, but some 13th and 14th century features are still visible. It contains two fine brasses of the early 14th century. The village PRIMARY SCHOOL was founded in 1842 by the Rev. Richard Dawes. It was an educational showpiece in its day, visited by such dignitaries as Lord Russell the Prime minister, Florence Nightingale, and Matthew Arnold. THE OLD VICARAGE is a Queen Anne building with an exceptional frontage. Possibly the oldest house in the village is CRUCK COTTAGE with the typical 'cruck' visible on its south elevation. There are some interesting farm workers cottages (no right of way) with an OAST HOUSE adjoining. There is a COMMEMORATIVE STONE to four German airmen whose aircraft was attacked at this point and crashed into a field near the Stockbridge road.

THE COWDROVE: This modest version of the ancient drove roads was used by travellers unwilling or unable to pay tolls on the 'new' Turnpike road to Stockbridge.

HURDLE MAKING: This ancient craft still continues in this area, depending on buying a large enough area of coppice each year to provide the necessary materials. The areas of coppice are known in this part of Hampshire as 'burls'.

Submitted by: Mr M Woodcock
6 Scott Close
Kings Somborne

WALK 9
AROUND BROUGHTON
– distance 9 miles (4½ hours)

Introduction
The area of this walk encompasses a Roman road, a Nature Conservation Area and the delightful villages of Broughton and Bossington, with long vistas over the Downland.

How to get there
Going north from Romsey on the A3057, Broughton will be found by turning left onto the B3084 three miles outside the town. If approaching from the Andover direction on the· A343, turn left onto the B3084 at Middle Wallop.

Points of Interest
BROUGHTON VILLAGE: In 1314 the then Rector was given an endowment in the form of a COLUMBARIUM (pigeon house). Its successor is now in the churchyard, a circular brick building with a conical roof dating from the time of William and Mary.

ST MARY'S CHURCH: Built in the early 13th century it boasts a beautiful stained glass window by Kempe in 1904.

WELL HEAD: This unusual construction in the High Street was sunk in 1921 after a severe drought.

ROMAN ROAD: The Sarum to Winchester road runs along the ridge south of the village.

ROUND BARROWS: On the southern edge of Broughton Down in the Whiteshoot Plantation are some fine barrows, one of which is 60ft in diameter and 6ft high.

BAPTIST CHAPEL: Is dated 1655 – surely one of the first generation of Baptists in the country.

BOSSINGTON HOUSE: Built in 1834 by John Davies , it is of a mellow yellow brick with shaped gables.

PITTLEWORTH MANOR: One mile south-west of

Bossington, it is famed for its room of Elizabethan wall paintings.

Submitted by: Rev. D. R. Howe
Broughton Rectory
Stockbridge

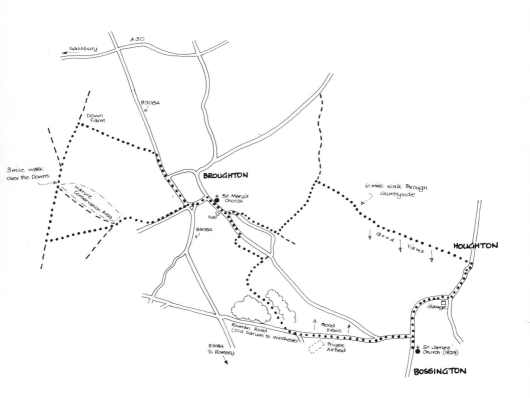

WALK 10
AROUND UPPER CLATFORD
– distance 3 miles (2 hours)

Introduction
Upper Clatford lies in a beautifully wooded valley and has
excellent views up and down the river Test. The route goes
through water meadows by the river Anton as well as passing
the watercress beds of Anna Valley.

How to get there
Upper Clatford lies just south of Andover off the A3057
Romsey road.

Points of Interest
ALL SAINTS CHURCH: Built 1100-1135 on the site of a Saxon
church, it was given by William the Conqueror to the convent
of Lire in Normandy. Here Roger, Earl of Arundel and
Shrewsbury gave Ardeline (a singer of whom he was
enamoured) a virgate (an old land measure, commonly 30
acres) of land. The church has some 17th century additions.
CLATFORD MANOR: ultimately went to Roger, Earl of
March and to Edward IV. At the Dissolution Henry VIII gave it
to Lord Berners, the translator of the works of Froissart.
WATERLOO IRON WORKS: Established in 1815, the
Ironmaster's House has been preserved as CLATFORD
LODGE. The lodges to the left and right of the archway were
built as school house and schoolmistress's house in 1836.
Waterloo Square, a group of worker's cottages, has now been
demolished.
POUNCEY'S FARM HOUSE: with its cottages are 18th
century buildings, although the farm was here before the
'Enclosure Awards'.
BURY HILL FORT: The three lines of banks and ditches which
crown the hill have been shown by excavation to belong to

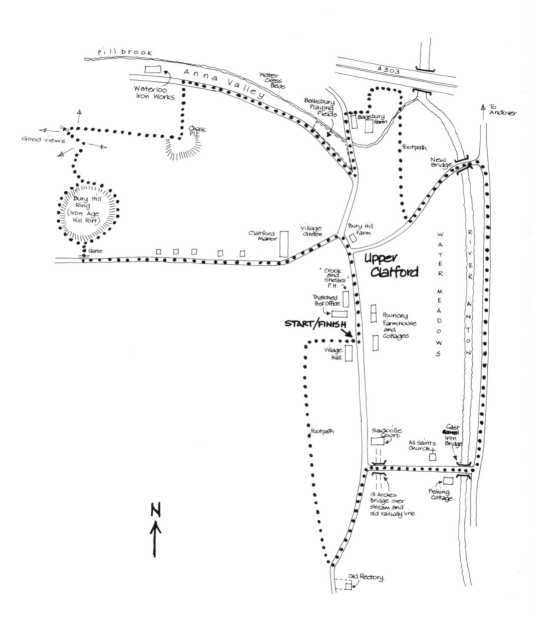

Pill brook

Anna Valley

Water Cress Beds

A 303

Waterloo Iron Works

Balksbury Playing Fields

Chalk Pit

Bagsbury Farm

Footpath

To Andover

Good views

New Bridge

Bury Hill Ring (Iron Age Hill Fort)

Clatford Manor

Village Green

Bury Hill Farm

W A T E R   M E A D O W S

R I V E R   A N T O N

Gate

Upper Clatford

"Crook and Shears" P.H.

Thatched Post Office

Pouncey Farmhouse and Cottages

START/FINISH

Village Hall

Footpath

Sackville Court

All Saints Church

Cast Iron Bridge

13 Arches Bridge over stream and old railway line

Fishing Cottage

N

Old Rectory

three distinct phases of occupation. Finds suggest intermittent habitation between 100 BC and 70 AD. The hill commands fine views to Quarley and the Downs to the north, and to Danebury in the south.

REDRICE HOUSE: Looking south from Bury Hill, the house lies in the distance, where General Webb, hero of Wynendael planted trees in avenues so as to represent the arrangement of Marlborough's troops at the battle of Malplaquet.

Submitted by: Mr D G Kennedy
'Sunraker'
Redrice Road
Upper Clatford
Andover

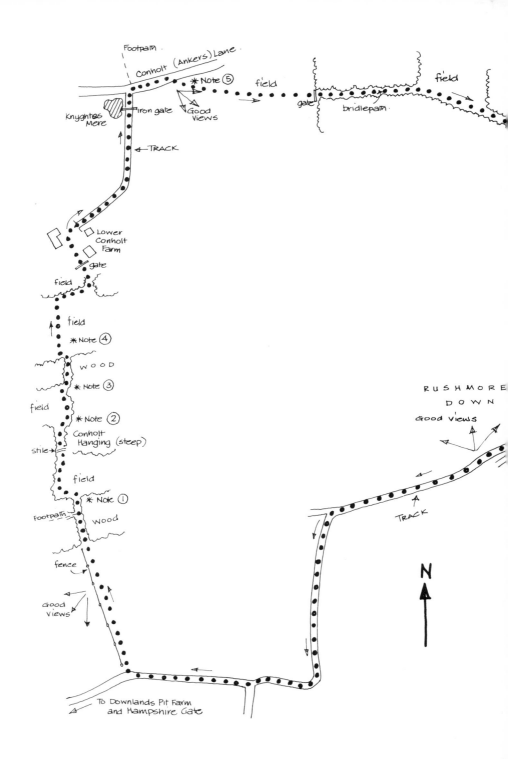

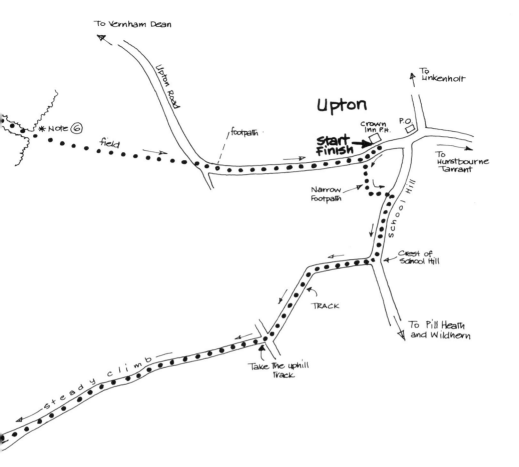

WALK 11
FROM THE CROWN INN, UPTON
– distance 5 miles (2½ hours)

Introduction

There are some commanding views of Rushmore Down and the North Hampshire Downs along this walk. The directional notes below are referred to by number on the map and will help guide the walker along the right track.

* Note 1. On leaving the wood, turn left 80 yds, then right along edge of field. Enter wood just right of iron gate over simple stile.
* Note 2. Continue along hedge on right.
* Note 3. Enter wood at small grass clearing slightly right of path line.
* Note 4. Keep to left edge and top edge of field.
* Note 5. Make for gap (gateway) in hedge 400 yds ahead.
* Note 6. On leaving wood, aim for grey barn about one mile away, then make for left-most of two gates at the bottom corner of the field.

How to get there

Upton is 2 miles north-west of Hurstbourne Tarrant, which lies north of Andover on the A343 Newbury road.

Points of Interest

KNYGHTES MERE: The Crusaders are alleged to have watered their horses here. This murky pond is always full.

HAMPSHIRE GATE: This is thought to have been the site of a gate to Savernake Forest when it was much larger.

DOWNLAND PIT FARM: once was a brick clay pit.

Submitted by: Mr J B W Birks
Long Meadow
Vernham Dean
Andover

WALK 12
AROUND KINGSCLERE
– distance 4 miles (2 hours)

Introduction
A circular walk around the village which includes all aspects
of ancient and modern Kingsclere: panoramic views, ancient

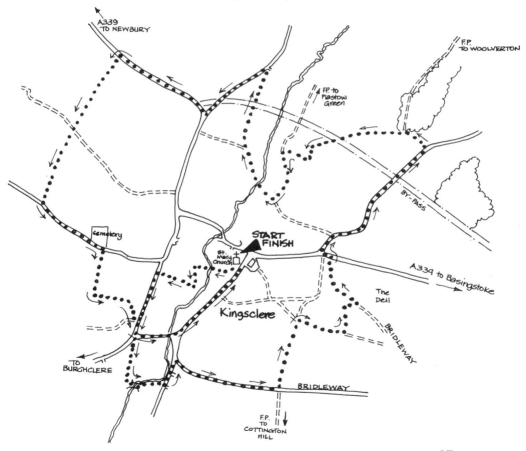

trackways, and beautiful paths beside the stream. There are several other paths that can be used to lengthen or shorten the walk.

How to get there
Kingsclere lies on the A339 Newbury to Basingstoke road. It can also be approached from the A34 Newbury to Southampton road.

Points of Interest
ST MARY'S CHURCH: Built 1130-1140 with many alterations over the centuries.
GAILEY MILL: existed in the 16th century. The causeway beside the stream was built by members of the Kingsclere Ramblers.
PARK HOUSE STABLES: once the home of the world famous Derby winner 'Mill Reef'. The downs above the village are used as gallops for the local trainers' horses and the area echoes the bloodstock country across the border into Berkshire.
COTTINGTON HILL: a land mark with the television mast.
THE DELL: an old chalk pit.
MILLS: Priors Mill was originally a Victorian mill, and Island Mill was once known as Lower Mill.
FROBIERY: 11th-12th century manor house.

Submitted by: Mrs M E Lawrence
29 Long Croft Road
Kingsclere

WALK 13
NEAR HARTLEY WINTNEY
– distance 3½ miles (1½ hours)

Introduction
Starting from West Green House, the route passes alongside a field containing some unusual species of animals including Llamas. A small detour to take in Dipley Mill is rewarding.

How to get there
Hartley Wintney lies on the A30 between Basingstoke .and Camberley. Turn off the A30 at Hartley Wintney on the Mattingley road to find the car park. Start Reference SU75-746544.

Points of Interest
HARTLEY WINTNEY: Voted best kept village in Hampshire in 1973, the trees which flourish on the green today were praised in 1821 by William Cobbett of *Rural Rides* fame as he passed by here. The village has a delightful church with a dignified peace memorial chapel to the dead of both World Wars.

WEST GREEN HOUSE: A very pretty house, Jacobean mainly, though the north and south sides date from 1905.

DUTCH HOUSE: Interesting style; three by three bays with giant pilaster-strips and mansard roof.

BRAMSHILL MANOR: Dominating the scene from its hill some two miles to the north of the walk, this magnificent Jacobean mansion sits like a castle in a fairy tale. There are references to a house here in the Domesday Book and Sir John Foxley and 'his manor of Bramshill' are mentioned in 1306. The surrounding countryside has a lot of gorse and broom, and it is the 'broom on the hill' which is thought to have given the mansion its name. It is one of the three claimants in

Hampshire to be the site of the Mistletoe Bough story. Briefly – this legend concerns the sad fate of a young bride, who during a game of hide and seek at the wedding celebrations hides in a wooden chest. The chest locks and the unfortunate bride, unable to attract the attention of the guests, meets her death.

Submitted by: Mr D N Beazley
'Datchets'
Cricket Green
Hartley Wintney

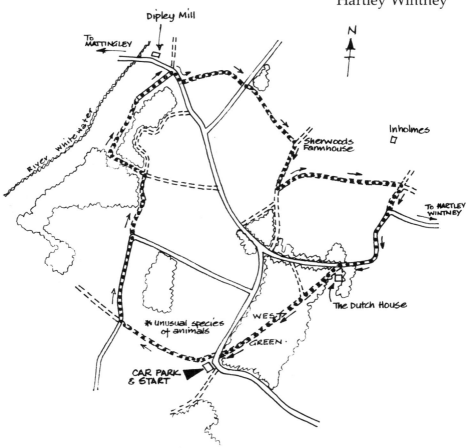

WALK 14
NEAR MEDSTEAD
– distance 3½ miles (2 hours)

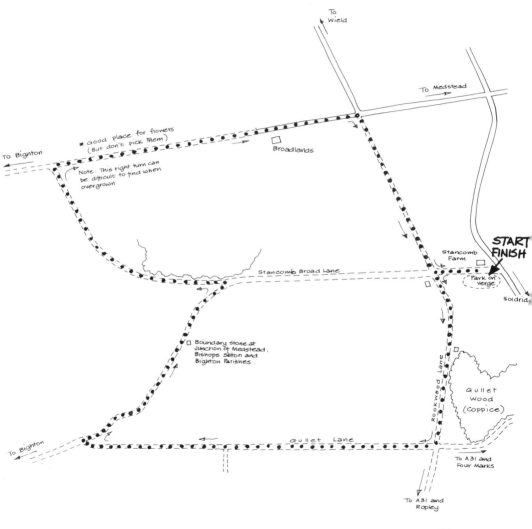

To Wield

To Medstead

To Bighton

* Good place for flowers
(But don't pick them)

Broadlands

Note: This right turn can be difficult to find when overgrown.

START FINISH

Stancomb Farm

Park on verge

Stancomb Broad Lane

Soldrid

☐ Boundary stone at junction of Medstead, Bishops Sutton and Bighton Parishes.

Rockwood Lane

Gullet Wood (Coppice)

To Bighton

Gullet Lane

To A31 and Four Marks

To A31 and Ropley

Introduction

This is a level walk on ancient trackways through fields and woodland. A wide variety of plants can be seen, including Solomon's Seal, Centaury, Mullein, Agrimony, Basil and Thyme. Also the area has many species of fungi.

How to get there

Medstead lies north of the A31 between Alton and New Alresford. Park on the grass verge opposite Stancombe Farm. Map reference 645350.

Points of Interest

STANCOMB BROAD LANE: This is a fine example of a green lane, some of its hedges could be more than 800 years old. It is possible that it formed part of an ancient route used by drovers.

GULLET WOOD: has been coppiced for many years. It can be seen by making a slight detour from the recommended route at Gullet Lane.

MEDSTEAD VILLAGE: Although fast becoming a suburb of Alton, the Old Village is picturesque. The church tower was a noted repository of smuggled goods, as was the vestry, since no one came near them during the week. The church also has an unusual poor box, thought to have been made in France about 500 years ago.

Submitted by: Mr D Gebbett
69 Blackberry Lane
Four Marks
Alton

WALK 15
AROUND LIPHOOK
AND WEAVERS DOWN
– distance 5 miles (2½ hours)

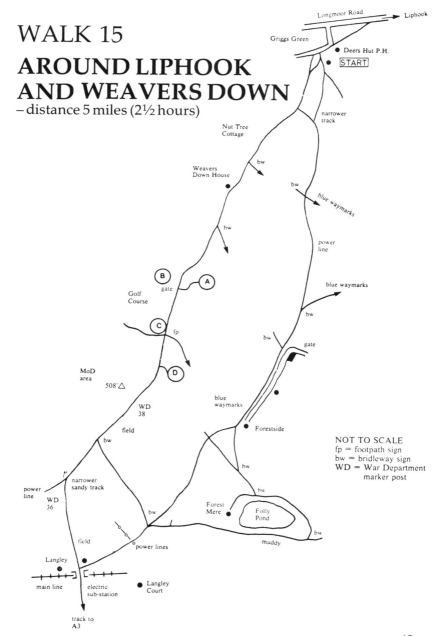

Longmoor Road

Liphook

Griggs Green

Deers Hut P.H.

START

narrower
track

Nut Tree
Cottage

Weavers
Down House

bw

bw

blue waymarks

power
line

blue waymarks

B   A

gate

bw

Golf
Course

C   fp

bw

gate

D

MoD
area

508°△

blue
waymarks

Forestside

NOT TO SCALE
fp = footpath sign
bw = bridleway sign
WD = War Department
        marker post

WD
38

field

bw

narrower
sandy track

bw   hw

power
line

WD
36

field

bw

Forest
Mere

Folly
Pond

hw

power lines

muddy

bw

Langley

main line   electric
             sub-station

Langley
Court

track to
A3

43

Introduction

A good any-season walk with excellent views of the Downs and Liphook. A mixture of bracken, birch and pine provide all-year colour. The route can be shortened by cutting off Langley loop, or extended by going round Folly Pond. The points on the map marked with a circle are worth the detour for a full panoramic view:-

(A) east to Foley Manor, Liphook, OSU, Bohunt School, Bramshott church.

(B) and (C) over new Kenwood golf course, Oakhanger radar station, Woolmer Forest and the North Downs.

(D) Folley Pond and Hydro, South Downs at Butser (better views can be had at trig point – but watch for the red flag).

How to get there

Liphook lies on the A3 Guildford to Petersfield road south of Hindhead. The start can be reached via the B2131 road west of the village.

Points of Interest

FOREST MERE: a large country house now a health hydro.

WEAVERS DOWN: uncultivated common land largely bracken, holly, birch and pine. Public access is limited to official rights of way.

KENWOOD COUNTRY CLUB: a major leisure complex completed in 1981. It includes indoor sports, a golf course, (reclaimed from bracken etc.), which is now partly Japanese owned.

MINISTRY OF DEFENCE LAND: To the west there is land within Longmoor Camp. Red flags warn when there may be danger, and various 'out of bounds' signs are there to warn Service personnel, not the public.

Submitted by: Mr D Clark
21 Chestnut Close
Liphook

WALK 16
FROM PETERSFIELD VIA RIDGE HANGER AND STEEP VILLAGE
– distance 6 miles (3 hours)

Introduction
This walk has excellent views of the surrounding Downs from Hanger Ridge, and also includes the waterfall at the end of Ashford Chase path, and the pretty field-path from Steep to Petersfield. The walk can be shortened at several points by using the quiet lanes. The Alton-Petersfield road is very busy and *not* recommended.

How to get there
Petersfield lies at the junction of the A3 Guildford to Portsmouth road and the A272 Winchester to Midhurst road. The walk begins in the town's Square.

Points of Interest
PETERSFIELD: The town received its first charter from William, Earl of Gloucester in the mid-12th century. Its prosperity was based on the wool and cloth trade, and being on the main London to Portsmouth road, it had a special hey-day during the coaching era, at one time its nine inns dealing with up to thirty coaches a day, which changed their horses here. The coach trade died dramatically when the Portsmouth to London railway opened in the late 19th century.
STATUE OF WILIAM III: stands in the Square, made under the will of Sir William Joliffe of Petersfield House. It originally stood in the grounds of that house, which was near the church and demolished in 1793.
ST PETER'S CHURCH: stands directly behind the monument and was built in the 12th century, although much restored.

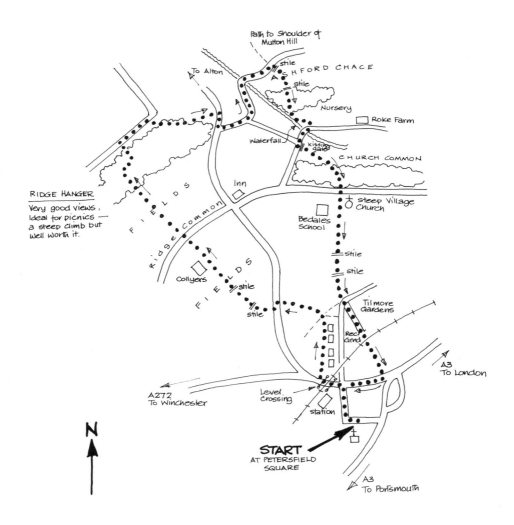

John Small, one of the Old Hambledon Cricket team (the cradle of the sport) and maker of its cricket balls lies buried in the churchyard.

BEDALES SCHOOL: Founded by John Haden Badley. In 1900 the school moved here from Sussex. It had quite advanced educational principles for the Victorian era of 'spare the rod, spoil the child' theory – his was a belief in freedom of thought and expression which represented a bold and unconventional educational experiment. The school's founder died in 1967 aged 102.

STEEP VILLAGE: Its church, All Saints, is early 13th century with a Victorian bell turret. There are some interesting houses, architecturally, to be seen, especially those designed by U F Unsworth in the early 20th century. The PLATTS is a prime example of his style.

SHOULDER OF MUTTON HILL: An excellent extension to the walk is to take the footpath and climb the very steep side of the hill. The far reaching views make it well worth the climb.

EDWARD THOMAS: On top of the Shoulder of Mutton Hill is a Sarsen Stone which forms a simple Memorial to the poet Edward Thomas who was killed in the Battle of Arras in 1917. The inscription on the stone reads 'And I rose up and knew I was tired, and continued my journey'.

Submitted by: Mr D Turland
52 Corbett Road
Waterlooville

WALK 17
AROUND DENMEAD AND HAMBLEDON
– distance 7 miles (3½ hours)

Introduction
Denmead lies among richly wooded peaceful downs in the neighbourhood of the Forest of Bere. The route is suitable for walking all year round.

How to get there
The walk begins at Denmead which is on the B2150. From the A3 Portsmouth to Petersfield road turn off at Waterlooville onto the B2150. From the west, leave the A32 Gosport to Alton road at Droxford onto the B2150.

Points of Interest
DENMEAD VILLAGE: is comparatively modern, being south-west of the original settlement, which was called Barn Green, Hambledon. Much of the village belonged to Ashling House, demolished in 1959. Among the most notable buildings to share the same fate over the past 50 years was the windmill that stood on the west side of what became Mill Road.

VINEYARD: The Downland soil is similar to that of the Champagne area of France, and the south-facing slopes get a generous share of sunshine. Major General Sir Guy Salisbury-Jones began the vineyard at Windmill Down in 1949. Today the 5 acres average about 8,000 bottles per season.

HAMBLEDON VILLAGE: This village has a pre-Conquest church. In 1199 the manor went to the Bishops of Winchester, remaining with them through the centuries until taken over by the Ecclesiastical Commission.

The village is famous as the 'cradle of cricket'. The Hambledon Cricket Club was founded about 1750. 'No eleven in England could compare with the Hambledon, which met on the first Tuesday in May on Broadhalfpenny'. The local team could and did beat teams picked from the whole of England.

FOREST OF BERE: Portsmouth has now expanded up and over Portsdown Hill, but looking south from the walk there was once a nine-mile wide belt of heath and forest stretching from Southampton to the Sussex border. It formed part of a Royal Forest in the time of William the Conqueror.

Submitted by: Mr B W Thomas
13 Hunters Ride
Waterlooville

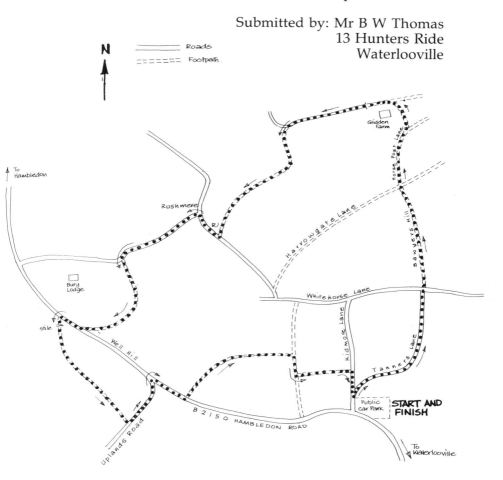

WALK 18
AROUND PORTSDOWN HILL
– distance 5 miles (2½ hours)

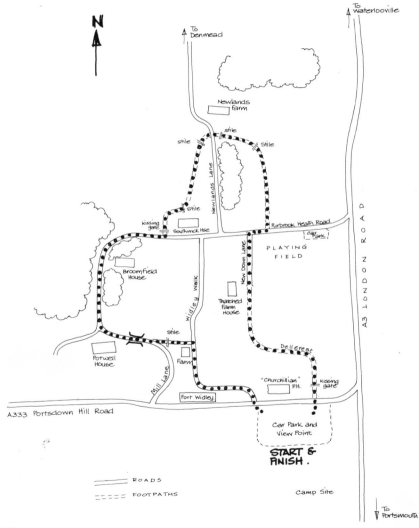

N

To Waterlooville

To Denmead

Newlands Farm

stile

stile

stile

Newlands Lane

stile

kissing gate

Southwick Hse

Purbrook Heath Road

Car Park

PLAYING FIELD

Broomfield House

Widley Walk

New Down Lane

Thatched Farm House

A3 LONDON ROAD

stile

Potwell House

Farm

Dellcrest

Mill Lane

"Churchillian" P.H.

kissing gate

Fort Widley

A333 Portsdown Hill Road

Car Park and View Point

START & FINISH.

———— ROADS

– – – – FOOTPATHS

Camp Site

To Portsmouth

Introduction

Portsdown's natural northern wall of chalk rises almost sheer from the developed coastal strip. From the car park view point there are excellent views of the Isle of Wight, Fawley to the west and Chichester to the east. There are extensive vistas north to Butser Hill, the Forest of Bere and the Meon Valley. The walk includes part of the Wayfarers Walk footpath from Emsworth to Newbury.

How to get there

The walk begins and ends just off the A3 London to Portsmouth Road.

Points of Interest

PORTSDOWN HILL: This natural cliff of chalk is crowned by the massive Palmerstonian forts and some mid-20th century installations. The older forts were built during the 1850s to guard the ports from any attack from the north. Therefore their strongest fortifications faced north, as it was feared that the French might land and gain command of the hill and thus threaten the dockyards with their mobile artillery.

FORT WIDLEY: Open April-September 1.30-5.30 (last tour 5.00 pm). It has a most perfect adaptation of profile to the hillside, so that from the north its form is almost invisible, with deep ditches cut into the hillside. There are hundreds of yards of deep tunnels through which the gunners were to be supplied with powder and shells from the underground arsenal. Visitors are able also to climb up on the roof of the barrack building for what is certainly the best view of Portsmouth, its harbour and Spithead.

Submitted by: Mr C H Holmes
14 Lugano Close
Waterlooville

WALK 19

AROUND MARWELL AND OWSLEBURY
– distance 3½ miles (1½ hours)

Introduction
An interesting walk, capable of variation, passing through the most attractive part of Owslebury village. Limited parking is available in the village.

How to get there
Owslebury lies to the east of the A333 Winchester to Portsmouth road.

Points of Interest
MARWELL PARK: dates back to the 1300s. The present house was largely rebuilt in 1815. It was the home of the Seymour family, and Henry VIII courted Jane Seymour here. It is said that great celebrations were held here when a chain of beacons were lit across the hills giving the news of Anne Boleyn's execution. Legend has it that the ghost of the tragic Anne haunts the Yew Park. MARWELL HALL is one of the claimants to be site of the tale of the Mistletoe Bough celebrated in poem by Samuel Rogers and ballad by Haynes Bailey. See also page 39 – Bramshill Manor.

MARWELL ZOOLOGICAL PARK: The estate was changed to a zoological park in 1972. It was the brain child of John Knowles and its abiding concern is for the survival and conservation of animal species threatened by extinction in the wild. It is well worth a visit.

BOYES FARM: was the scene of a disturbance during the Labourers' Revolt of the 1830s. Their protest against the introduction of the new threshing machines culminated in the 'Swing Riots'. The mythical Captain Swing was said to responsible for machine breaking throughout the south of

England. The revolts were vigorously suppressed by the authorities.

ST ANDREW'S CHURCH: This seems to have been altered on several occasions in the 17th century. One guide book describes it rather unkindly as having been 'tinkered up by successive vicars with more zeal than taste'.

SHIP INN: is said to have been constructed from ships' timbers.

Submitted by: Mr D Knapp
Woods Cottage
Hensting
Fishers Pond
Eastleigh

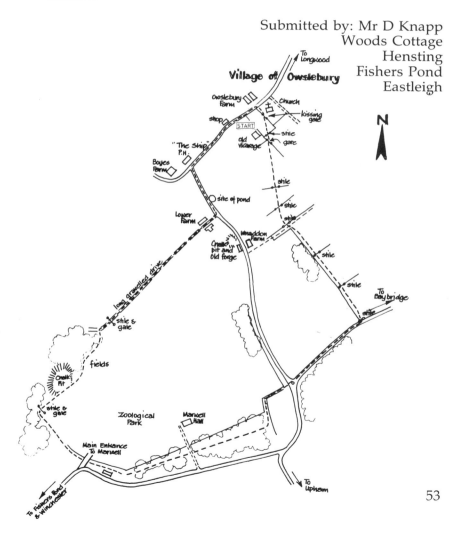

53

WALK 20

AROUND THE LONGWOOD ESTATE NEAR OWSLEBURY

– distance 4 miles (1½ hours)

Introduction

The route is fairly level, going through arable farmland and some very attractive woodland.

How to get there

The Longwood Estate lies to the north of Owslebury off the A333 Winchester to Portsmouth road. It can also be approached on the B3035 from Winchester.

Points of Interest

LONGWOOD ESTATE: In recent years it was run as a shooting estate, though originally LONGWOOD HOUSE was one of the two manors of Owslebury. Now owned by the Transport and General Workers Union it is managed as an arable farm, with some sheep and still a little shooting.

Nearby is the village of Owslebury which has some interesting features (see Walk 19).

Submitted by: Mr D Knapp
Woods Cottage
Hensting
Fishers Pond
Eastleigh

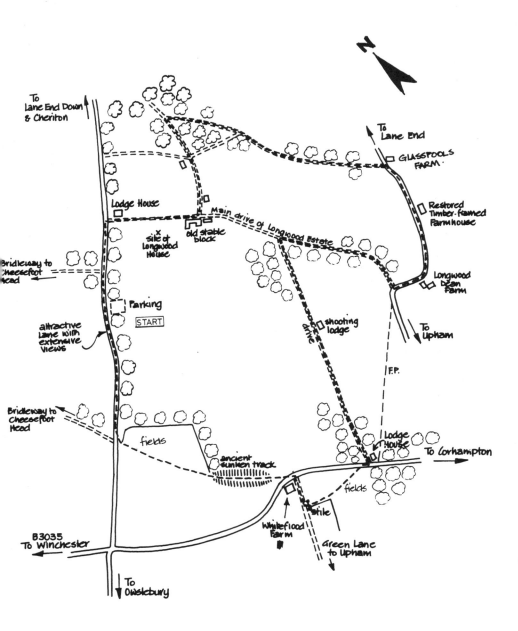

To
Lane End Down
& Cheriton

To
Lane End

GLASSPOOLS
FARM.

Lodge House

Main drive of Longwood Estate

Restored
Timber-framed
Farmhouse

x
site of
Longwood
House

old stable
block

Bridleway to
cheesefoot
head

Longwood
Dean
Farm

To
Upham

Parking

START

shooting
lodge

drive

attractive
lane with
extensive
views

F.P.

Bridleway to
cheesefoot
head

fields

Lodge
House

To Corhampton

ancient
sunken track

fields

B3035
To Winchester

Whitefield
Farm

stile

Green Lane
to Upham

To
Owslebury

55

WALK 21
AT CHEESEFOOT HEAD
– distance 5 miles (2½ hours)

Introduction
Circular route from Cheesefoot Head with open views of
mostly arable land, ranging north to Berkshire, south to the
Isle of Wight, east to Sussex and west to Winchester and
beyond.

How to get there
The car park and start lie two miles from Winchester on the
A272 Petersfield road.

Submitted by: Mrs K Coxhead
9 Hanover Lodge
St Cross Road
Winchester

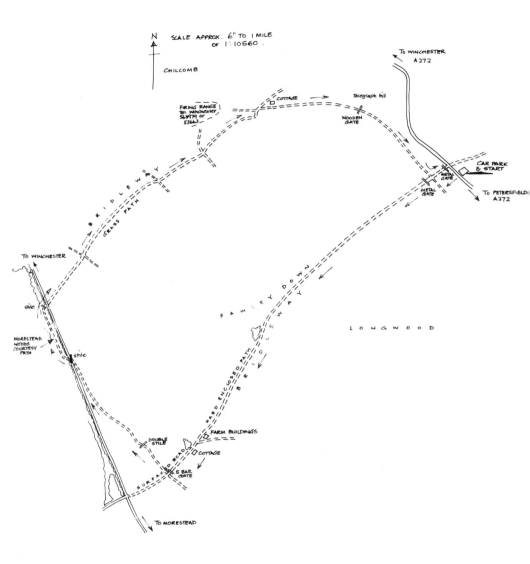

N

SCALE APPROX. 6" TO 1 MILE
or 1:10560.

CHILCOMB

To WINCHESTER
A272

CHILCOMB

COTTAGE

Telegraph Hill

FIRING RANGE
Tel. Winchester
564979 or
53663

WOODEN
GATE

CAR PARK
& START

METAL
GATE

METAL
GATE

To PETERSFIELD
A272

B R I D L E W A Y

GRASS PATH

TO WINCHESTER

stile

MORESTEAD
WOODS
COURTESY
PATH

stile

F A W L E Y   D O W N

B R I D L E   W A Y

L O N G W O O D

HARD ENCLOSED PATH

DOUBLE
STILE

FARM BUILDINGS

SURFACED ROAD

COTTAGE

5 BAR
GATE

TO MORESTEAD

57

WALK 22
AROUND ABBOTSTONE DOWN
– distance 3½ miles (2 hours)

Introduction
A pleasant walk through agricultural land following footpaths and bridleways, affording fine views of the surrounding countryside. Abbotstone Down comprises one of the last remaining fragments of downland plateau in the county, and supports a surprising wealth of flora. For example there are 56 varieties of mosses and liverwort which have been identified. Part of the walk forms a portion of the Wayfarers Walk long distance footpath from Emsworth to Newbury.

How to get there
The car park and start at Abbotstone Down lies on the B3046 between Basingstoke to the north and New Alresford to the south.

Points of Interest
BOTTOM COPSE: The word copse is derived from coppice. This copse, plus Thorngrove copse close by, are typical of such small woods which now consist of overgrown hazel coppice. Today coppicing is judged uneconomic and these woods are increasingly grubbed out in favour of forestry plantation or arable cultivation. The 32 acres of Abbotstone Down were purchased by the County Council to be preserved and managed as natural woodland, downland and scrub.

Submitted by: Mr E F Nicholl
Tannery Cottage
Ladywell Lane
Alresford

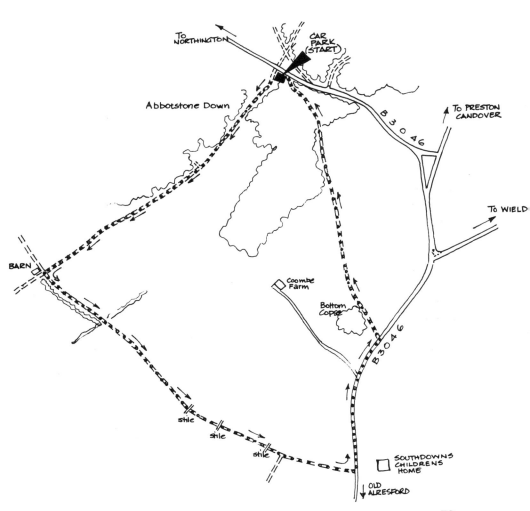

N

TO
NORTHINGTON

CAR
PARK
(START)

Abbotstone Down

B 3 0 4 6

TO PRESTON
CANDOVER

TO WIELD

BARN

Coombe
Farm

Bottom
Copse

B 3 0 4 6

stile

stile

stile

SOUTHDOWNS
CHILDRENS
HOME

OLD
ALRESFORD

59

WALK 23
MICHELDEVER
– distance 6 miles (3 miles)

Introduction
An easy walk through fields and beechwoods, passing through Micheldever village with its attractive old thatched cottages and interesting church.

How to get there
Micheldever lies just to the west of the A33 Winchester to Basingstoke road, south of North Waltham.

Points of Interest
COFFIN WALK: An old route taken to bring coffins for burial from East Stratton to Micheldever churchyard.
EMPTY DITCH: Originally dug on the orders of Lord Rank for training his gun dogs.
ST MARY'S CHURCH: The tower is early 16th century, and it has an unusual octagonal nave, dated 1890. One of the famous names to be remembered in the church is the Baring family, originally from Austria, who settled at BARING STRATTON PARK near Micheldever. In the 18th century

Francis Baring became one of Europe's leading businessmen and financiers, and chairman of the East India Company. His son was created Lord Ashburton.

THE CREASE: important crossways in medieval times.

MICHELDEVER STATION: Railway travellers will know Micheldever best for its series of long tunnels excavated beneath some of Hampshire's highest land, the POPHAM BEACONS. These were an impresssive feat of the Victorian engineer Joseph Locke.

Submitted by: Mr P Whitfield
Micheldever Parish Council

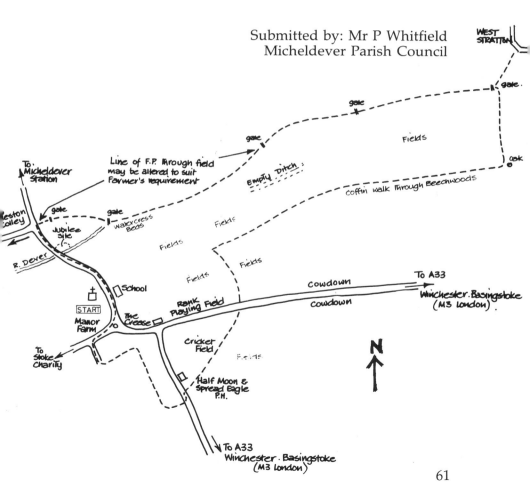

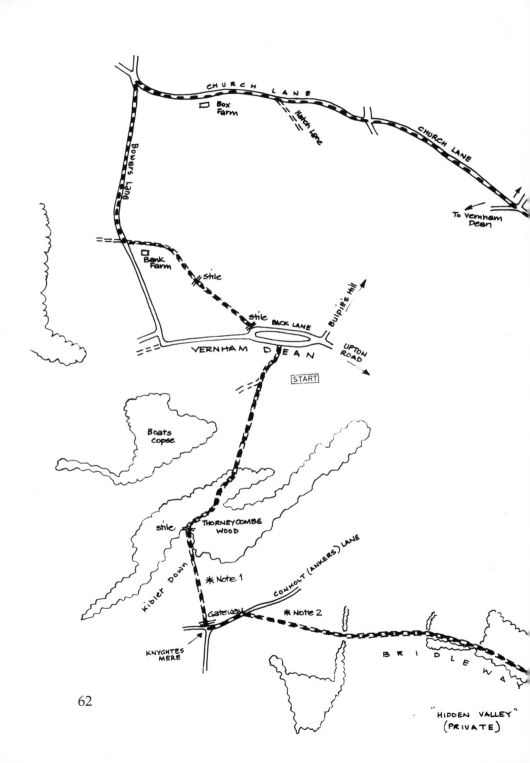

WALK 24
AROUND VERNHAM DEAN
– distance 6 miles (3 hours)

Introduction
The route is in a very pretty area with fields and woodlands sloping up towards the border with Berkshire and Wiltshire. There are directional notes numbered on the map to guide the walker:

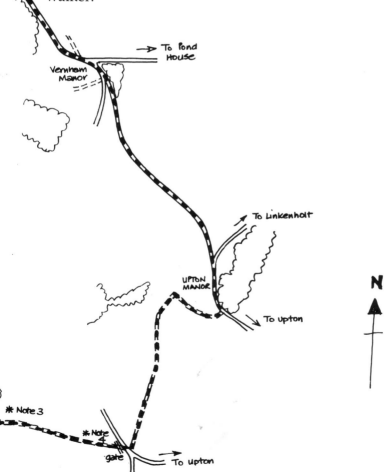

Directional notes –

* Note 1 Walking away from Vernham Dean aim for the highest point of the field, then look for the gateway. Towards Vernham Dean aim for far left corner of field.

* Note 2 Make for gap (gateway) in hedge 400 yards ahead.

* Note 3 Aim for grey barn about 1 mile away, then make for left-most of two gates at the bottom corner of the field.

* Note 4 Aim for the highest point of the field then for a gap at the top of the wood on the right.

Points of Interest

ST MARY'S CHURCH: The nave, chancel and bellcote date from 1220. The rest of the building is of 1851, 'the design of the curate Rev J.M. Rawlins'. The distance between the church and village in this scattered community reflects a story of the Great Plague. Legend has it that the then rector persuaded the villagers to gather in a remote spot while he ostensibly went to Andover for help, but in reality to escape. Alas, he was infected and died while still on Vernham Hill, leaving his ghost to haunt it to this day.

Submitted by: Mr J B W Birks
Long Meadow
Vernham Dean
Andover